The CRANE and the KEEPER

The CRANE and the KEEPER

How an Endangered Crane Chose a Human as Her Mate

Meeg Pincus

ILLUSTRATED BY

Gillian Eilidh O'Mara

 Smithsonian kids

 CANDLEWICK ENTERTAINMENT

Walnut the white-naped crane had a problem. A big problem.
At twenty-four years old, she was being sent away from her zoo
home. The same thing had happened at her last two zoos.
And no other zoo would take her.

You see, Walnut was usually a cheerful, curious crane—
prone to dancing. But when keepers put her with other cranes,
especially potential mates, she'd lash out like a lion.
There were whispers that she'd slashed at
two suitors with her sharp bill!

What made Walnut cast aside other cranes?
Well, she may have looked like a crane. She may have
moved, eaten, and called like a crane. But in her mind,
she was not a crane.

She was human.

How does a crane come to think that she's human? It happens at hatching . . . as it did for Walnut. On a sweltering Wisconsin summer day in 1981, she hatched in an old horse barn. She was greeted by volunteers, whose group had rescued her parents after poachers stole them from the wild. The volunteers named her after the local diner's popular walnut pie.

One of them must have cared for Walnut extra kindly, like a loving parent. Maybe they cuddled her and cooed at her, as if she were a human baby. This might sound nice. But little did they know then that this touching and tenderness leads to terrible trouble for a crane chick.

A trouble called imprinting.

Some species of animals, including cranes, imprint on their first caretakers. As babies, they cling closely and attach for life, which helps keep them safe in the wild.

But when that first caretaker is from a different species, an imprinted baby comes to see itself as a member of *that* species, instead of its own.

Animals imprinted on different-species caretakers often grow up to snub same-species mates. They never have babies—or as scientists say, *breed*.

Walnut became imprinted on humans. But not breeding wouldn't work for her . . . because she was no ordinary white-naped crane.

Wildlife scientists said she was the most important white-naped crane on earth!

Harmful human habits were swiftly shrinking Walnut's species. And the few white-naped cranes in zoos were related to one another. So their genes—which pass down traits from parents to offspring—were too similar to carry on the species in a healthy way. With her wild-caught parents, though, Walnut had the perfect genes to do so.

Thus, the big problem: Walnut was the most strongly imprinted crane her keepers had ever seen. She'd attacked every mate presented to her. But she *needed* to hatch chicks to save her species!

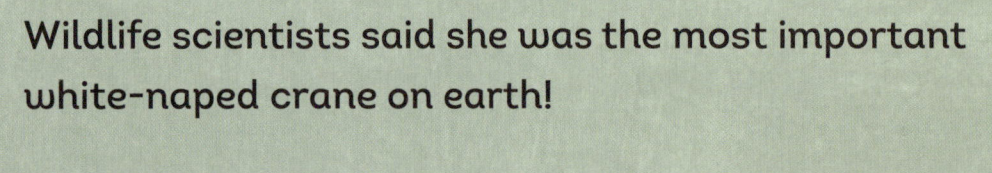

Who could help her now?

Luckily, there was one last hope—a special breeding program for endangered cranes in the rolling foothills of Virginia. The Smithsonian's National Zoo and Conservation Biology Institute (NZCBI) agreed to give Walnut a chance.

But her case would be a tough nut to crack. A case NZCBI would hand over to its newly hired crane keeper.

Chris Crowe, just four years older than Walnut, had a bird-friendly last name and a big job to do. Five days a week, he would care for and help breed seventeen endangered cranes . . . including one bold new arrival who thought she was human.

Could this young wildlife keeper help Walnut save the white-naped cranes?

Some might say Chris Crowe was born to save species.
Growing up among Maryland's ash trees and pines,
he marveled at every squirrel, bird, and frog.

Once, on a vacation to Yellowstone National Park, his family spotted a wild bison.

Chris stared at the bison's warm, brown eyes . . . shiny, wet nose . . . soft, twitching ears.

He felt a connection, heartbeat to heartbeat, being to being. Then he learned that humans had nearly killed off the entire bison species.

A thought rang through his young mind, loud and clear as a bison's bellow: *If humans harm wildlife species, then humans must save them.*

And Chris decided he would be someone who saves them.

True to his word, Chris grew up to study wildlife species conservation.

He worked with red wolves, piping plovers, and California condors. He had also worked with whooping cranes—rearing chicks, just as Walnut had been raised by her rescuers.

But the big difference by the time Chris became a keeper was that wildlife science had settled on strategies to avoid imprinting. So Chris wore a crane costume to hide his humanness. He avoided eye contact with the chicks. And he didn't speak, only trilled and purred as a crane parent would.

All that experience with endangered species brought Chris Crowe to his new job at NZCBI—and face-to-face with Walnut.

When Walnut first met Chris, she crouched and circled. She hunched her head and fluffed her crown feathers. She waved her wings and lunged at her new keeper's legs.

Threat displays! This was not going to be easy.

Chris stuck a warning sign on Walnut's enclosure. He knew it wasn't safe to pair her with any of the endangered male cranes. He'd have to breed Walnut using science—with injections containing genetic material that would allow her to lay eggs without a mate.

And to do that, he would need to earn her trust.

(CAUTION)
AGGRESSIVE
CRANE

Mice. Mealworms. Peanuts. Grapes. For many months, Chris tempted Walnut with her favorite treats. She took his tasty bribes . . . but gave him the stink eye in return.

Walnut wasn't exactly afraid of Chris. Unlike the other cranes, she'd strut her twelve-pound self over to him and watch him work. He couldn't approach her, though, or she'd dart away.

Nearly two years into their time together, Walnut began to make new displays toward Chris. She bobbed her head, leaped, and ran around with her wings flapping. She trumpeted and grabbed grass, sticks, and flowers and tossed them in the air.

Chris wasn't exactly sure what he was watching. So he closely studied the displays of NZCBI's crane pairs. Sure enough, the females would bob, leap, flap, trumpet, and toss. The males would respond in turn. Then they'd make their nests together.

Could Walnut be . . . courting Chris as a mate?

With his commitment to conservation, Chris was willing to sometimes look silly. If he had to act like a bird again to save a species, he'd act like a bird.

So Chris bobbed his head at Walnut. He leaped, flapped his arms, trumpeted the best he could, and tossed grass, sticks, and flowers her way.

He knew that if Walnut trusted him, he could safely breed her with injections. But he hadn't thought before that she might actually see him as a potential mate. When cranes are mated, they're happier, live longer, and breed better. Was it possible that Walnut—human imprinted as she was—could choose a man for a mate?

Maybe not. At Chris's first awkward antics . . .

she turned up her beak.

Still, over the next year, some signs pointed to a possible connection. When Chris returned from vacations, Walnut acted aloof, like a house cat with hurt feelings—clearly unhappy with his absence. When snowstorms hit, the other cranes scattered stressfully, but Walnut waited calmly in the food shed for Chris to show up and shovel her out.

Her threat displays slowly stopped. Was she starting to trust him?

Over more months, Walnut slowly showed Chris what she wanted from him. She liked specific types and sizes of nesting materials and disliked others. She liked when he approached her slowly and tossed her a mouse.

Walnut stopped being mad at Chris for leaving . . . and started dancing when he returned. One step at a time, she started to let him touch her, and then pet her on her back.

Finally, it grew clear: Walnut had chosen Chris as her mate. And she was ready to breed.

After years of Chris's patient trust-building, breeding Walnut became easy. A simple injection, calmly accepted, allowed Walnut to lay a fertilized egg—a precious gift for her shrinking species!

Because an imprinted crane can't properly parent chicks, Chris passed Walnut's eggs to NZCBI's crane pairs. He left Walnut wooden eggs, the usual decoy, to nest on instead. But she wasn't buying it—she bumped them out and even buried one. Then Chris hatched an idea: he drained a real unfertilized crane egg and filled it with plaster. Walnut nested like a mama on that! And Chris stopped by to give her breaks to eat, stretch her legs, and bathe in the creek.

Slowly, this unlikely pair figured out how to work together.

Walnut had seven surviving offspring over eleven years, doing something extraordinary for her species. Even after she retired from breeding, Walnut would still build a nest with Chris each year. He would toss her mice and leave her peanuts, grapes, and mealworms. She would wait for him in the shed when it snowed.

Walnut passed away in January 2024 at the age of 42.
She had spent nearly twenty years at NZCBI with Chris.

Walnut's chicks are all grown up, with mates and chicks of their own—carrying on new generations of white-naped cranes.

With a little help and understanding,
Walnut solved her big problem—finding
the right home and mate for herself.

And with much determination, Chris Crowe
accomplished his big job—upholding his
lifelong belief:

*If humans harm wildlife species,
then humans must save them.*

More About Walnut

July 1981–January 2024

Birthplace: Baraboo, Wisconsin (International Crane Foundation barn)

Parents: Mercury and Amazon (captured illegally in China, rescued by local authorities, and sent to the International Crane Foundation in the United States)

Species: White-naped crane

Feather Colors: White, black, gray, red

Eye Color: Red

Weight: 12 pounds (5.4 kilograms)

Height: 4 feet (1.2 meters) (Cranes are the tallest of all flying birds.)

Personality Traits: Friendly, curious, bold, loyal

Diet: Natural diet: seeds, roots, plants, grains, insects, rodents, amphibians. Treats: peanuts, mealworms, grapes.

Residences: Denver Zoo; Cincinnati Zoo and Botanical Garden; Memphis Zoo; Smithsonian's National Zoo & Conservation Biology Institute (NZCBI) in Front Royal, Virginia

Keeper (Mate): Chris Crowe (human)

Breeding Method: Artificial insemination (injection of donor sperm from a male crane)

Number of Chicks: 7

Number of Grandchicks: 6 and counting

More About White-Naped Cranes

Conservation Status: Vulnerable (estimated 6,700 to 7,700 in the wild, according to the International Crane Foundation)

Native Habitat: Grassy marshes and wetlands

Native Territory: China, Mongolia, and Russia; with migrations south to Korea and Japan

Life Span: Unknown in the wild; in human care, median 15 years, oldest known 45 years

More About Cranes

The 15 Crane Species: Black-crowned, black-necked, blue, brolga, demoiselle, Eurasian, gray-crowned, hooded, red-crowned, sandhill, sarus, Siberian, wattled, white-naped, whooping

Wingspan: 5 to 8 feet (1.5 to 2.5 meters) (depending on species)

Weight: 4 to 22 pounds (2 to 10 kilograms) (depending on species)

Conservation Status: The International Crane Foundation describes cranes as being among the most endangered families of birds in the world, with eleven species under threat of extinction.

Top Threats to Cranes: Habitat/wetlands loss (due to human development, fires, livestock grazing, climate change, and pollution); poisoning; hunting and poaching

Crane Predators: Raccoons, foxes, coyotes, eagles, and humans

Strategies to Save Cranes: Habitat conservation and restoration; education

Migration Patterns: Migrate yearly for wintering

Mating Patterns: Unison calls, dancing displays, rarely lose sight of each other, share egg incubating duties. If one mate dies, the other may stop eating and/or make mournful calls for weeks.

Life Span: Up to 30 years in the wild; up to 45 years in human care

More About Animal Imprinting

What is animal imprinting?

Imprinting is when certain animals align their species identity with their early caretaker(s). It occurs in the first two weeks of life (identifying with "parents") and strengthens if the animals are away from their own species as they mature (identifying potential mates). Once animals are imprinted in both of those life stages, like Walnut, the imprinting is permanent and irreversible.

What animal species imprint?

Mostly bird species imprint—cranes, owls, ducks, geese, turkeys, penguins, chickens, and others. A few species of mammals—which, like birds, are also early walkers (called precocial) and need to find their mothers out of large groups—have similar types of strong bonding with early caretakers. Raccoons, pandas, guinea pigs, hyenas, and zebras, for example, bond quickly and strongly with their early caretakers, whatever their species. But scientists usually call this habituation, rather than imprinting, as those animals can rebond with their own species, while strongly imprinted birds do not.

Why can imprinting and habituation be bad?

Imprinting and habituation of wild animals to humans can be dangerous for the animals and the people. In the wild, fear of humans protects animals from getting too close to buildings and vehicles, keeping them away from human harm. As with Walnut, imprinting can also prevent animals from breeding, which can mean not carrying on a species. Imprinted animals often don't "fit in" with their own species or their imprinted species. It can also be dangerous for humans when wild animals lose their fear of people, as they can become aggressive.

How can imprinting and habituation be avoided?

Over the past thirty years, wildlife scientists have discovered successful strategies to help animal conservation programs avoid imprinting and habituation, especially for animals that are slated to be returned to the wild. These animal-teaching strategies include noise-making (recorded and/or mimicked, to sound like or to scare), use of costumes and/or puppets (to look like parent animals), and avoiding eye contact (to prevent human connection with the animals).

Q&A with Chris Crowe, Animal Keeper and Conservation Biologist

What did you study in school to become an animal keeper/conservation biologist?

I studied ecology (the relationship between animals and their natural habitats), ornithology (the study of birds), and other life sciences and earned a degree in wildlife science. Most keepers have bachelor's and/or master's degrees in biology, zoology, or other related fields.

What qualities does one need to be a good—or even great—animal keeper?

Good observation skills and a strong sense of responsibility are the keys to making sure zoo animals are happy, healthy, and living their best life in human care. The ability to communicate well with my fellow keepers, scientists, veterinarians, and the general public is essential. Keepers often spend a lot of time on our feet, lifting heavy objects or stooping to fix things, so it helps to be handy and have good stamina.

What do you enjoy most about working with animals, especially birds?

Getting to know the individual personalities of birds and earning their trust, especially Walnut's, is the most enjoyable part of my job. It is exciting, too, when birds have and raise young, providing a boost to rare species populations and hope for those of us trying to save them.

I want to work with animals! What are your tips for getting started?

Read as much as you can about the behavior and natural history of animals. Learn observation skills by sitting quietly and watching local birds and squirrels. Get hands-on experience by volunteering or interning at your local animal sanctuary, wildlife rehabilitation center, or zoo.

I want to help birds at home! What can I do?

Warn birds about windows by breaking up the reflections of sky and trees on them with temporary paint or other treatments. Avoid using pesticides (birds eat bugs!) or other chemicals, and plant native plants and trees. Keep your pet cat indoors; they can sneak up on and harm birds, especially those that feed or nest on the ground.

More About NZCBI (and the Bird House!)

The Smithsonian's National Zoo and Conservation Biology Institute (NZCBI) was founded in 1889 and now includes the Smithsonian's National Zoo, a public 163-acre park in Washington, DC; the Smithsonian Conservation Biology Institute, a 3,200-acre campus in Front Royal, Virginia; and field research stations and training sites worldwide. NZCBI's two main campuses today are home to more than two thousand animals, including some of the planet's most critically endangered species. NZCBI aims to save wildlife species from extinction and train future generations of conservationists. Visit: https://nationalzoo.si.edu/conservation.

The National Zoo is also home to the Bird House. Originally opened in 1928, the exhibit reopened after renovation in 2023 as a one-of-a-kind experience to celebrate and learn about birds, their migrations, and their conservation. It features nearly one hundred species of birds—including shorebirds, waterfowl, and songbirds—in walk-through aviaries, as well as hands-on exhibits and a bird-tracking lab. Visit: https://nationalzoo.si.edu/animals/exhibits/bird-house.

For Further Exploration

Websites

American Bird Conservancy: https://abcbirds.org

The Cornell Lab of Ornithology: www.birds.cornell.edu/home

The International Crane Foundation: https://savingcranes.org

The National Audubon Society: www.audubon.org

The Smithsonian Migratory Bird Center: https://nationalzoo.si.edu/migratory-birds

Books for Young Readers

D'Aquino, Andrea. *She Heard the Birds: The Story of Florence Merriam Bailey*. Hudson, NY: Princeton Architectural Press, 2022.

Frost, Helen. *Hello, I'm Here!* Photographs by Rick Lieder. Somerville, MA: Candlewick, 2019.

McClure, Wendy. *A Garden to Save the Birds.* Illustrated by Beatriz Mayumi. Chicago: Albert Whitman, 2021.

McCollough, Joy. *Harriet's Ruffled Feathers: The Woman Who Saved Millions of Birds.* Illustrated by Romina Galotta. New York: Atheneum, 2022.

Rose, Deborah Lee, and Jane Veltkamp. *Beauty and the Beak: How Science, Technology, and a 3D-Printed Beak Rescued a Bald Eagle.* Ithaca, NY: Persnickety Press, 2017.

Semple, Heidi E.Y. *Counting Birds: The Idea That Helped Save Our Feathered Friends.* Illustrated by Clover Robin. Lake Forest, CA: Seagrass/Quarto, 2018.

Ward, Jennifer. *How to Find a Bird.* Illustrated by Diana Sudyka. New York: Beach Lane, 2020.

Audiovisual Resource

Watch a video of Walnut and Chris! https://youtu.be/UK4KCEpXdZ0

Bibliography

Chorney, Saryn. "Bird 'Bachelorette': Meet the Rare Female Crane Who Chose a Man Named Crowe as Her Mate for Life." *People*, August 2, 2018. https://people.com/pets/walnut -crane-zookeeper-chris-crowe-mate-for-life-smithsonian-zoo/.

Crowe, Chris. Interviews with author. November 17, 2021. June 22, 2022.

Dingfelder, Sadie. "The Crane Who Fell in Love with a Human." *Washington Post*, July 23, 2018. https://www.washingtonpost.com/news/style/wp/2018/07/23/feature/the-crane-who -fell-in-love-with-a-human/.

Duerr, Rebecca S., and Laurie J. Gage, eds. *Hand-Rearing Birds*. 2nd ed. Hoboken, NJ: Wiley-Blackwell, 2020.

"Frequently Asked Questions About Cranes." International Crane Foundation. https://savingcranes.org/learn/frequently-asked-questions-about-cranes/.

Funnell, Rachael. "The Zoo Keeper Who 'Fathered' Five Chicks with a Murderous Endangered Crane." *IFL Science*, October 8, 2021. https://www.iflscience.com/the-zoo-keeper-who -fathered-five-chicks-with-a-murderous-endangered-crane-61218.

Gee, George F., David H. Ellis, and Claire M. Mirande. *Cranes: Their Biology, Husbandry, and Conservation*. Blaine, WA: Hancock House, 1996.

Greene, Patricia. "8 Types of Animals That Imprint (with Pictures)." Wildlife Informer. https://wildlifeinformer.com/animals-that-imprint/.

"Human Imprinting in Birds and the Importance of Surrogacy." Wildlife Center of Virginia. https://www.wildlifecenter.org/human-imprinting-birds-and-importance-surrogacy.

"Imprinting." Biology Online, Dictionary. https://www.biologyonline.com/dictionary/ imprinting.

"White-naped Crane." International Crane Foundation. https://savingcranes.org/learn /species-field-guide/white-naped-crane/.

"White-naped crane." Smithsonian's National Zoo & Conservation Biology Institute. https://nationalzoo.si.edu/animals/white-naped-crane.

"Who's Your Mama? The Science of Imprinting." PBS, *Nature*, November 16, 2012. https://www .pbs.org/wnet/nature/my-life-as-a-turkey-whos-your-mama-the-science-of -imprinting/7367/.

Glossary

breed: to produce offspring, or babies

conservation: protection of an animal or plant species or of a natural environment

courting: behaving in a way to attract a mate

decoy: an object that looks like another object and is used in place of it

display: movements and sounds an animal makes to communicate something, such as a warning (threat display) or a desire to breed (courting display)

endangered: at risk; used in reference to animal or plant species to mean at risk of becoming extinct

fertilized egg: an egg containing material that is capable of developing into an individual offspring

gene: the basic unit of a body's DNA code that passes traits from parent to child

generation: a group of individuals born around the same time

genetic material: a substance that contains genes

imprinting: the natural process by which wild animal young attach for life to their first caretakers

injection: a shot; a way to transfer fluids into a body using a syringe

mate: a partner; a member of a breeding pair

offspring: the young of an animal or plant

poacher: a person who breaks the law by stealing wild animals or plants from their natural habitat

species: a group of animals or plants of the same kind with the same name

To my first caretakers, my parents,
for teaching me to be a lifelong learner and reader.
And to all the people dedicating their lives
to conserving wildlife.
MP

For Oakleaf Community,
the best "found family" my own
little chicks and I could ask for
GEO

First edition 2025

Library of Congress Catalog Card Number pending
ISBN 978-1-5362-3236-3

24 25 26 27 28 29 CCP 10 9 8 7 6 5 4 3 2 1

Printed in Shenzhen, Guangdong, China

This book was typeset in Intro Book.
The illustrations were created digitally.

Candlewick Entertainment
an imprint of
Candlewick Press
99 Dover Street
Somerville, Massachusetts 02144

www.candlewick.com